4/2017

....

From Mother to Daughter

....

From Mother to Daughter

Advice and Lessons for a Good Life

Sherry Appel

ST. MARTIN'S GRIFFIN
New York

FROM MOTHER TO DAUGHTER. Copyright © 1995, 2017 by Sherry Appel. All rights reserved. Printed in the United States of America. For information, address St. Martin's Press, 175 Fifth Avenue, New York, N.Y. 10010.

www.stmartins.com

Designed by Sara Stemen

The Library of Congress has cataloged the first edition as follows:

Appel, Sherry Conway.
  From mother to daughter: advice and lessons for a good life / Sherry Conway Appel.
    p. cm.
  ISBN 0-312-13498-3 (hardcover)
  1. Women—Quotations, maxims, etc. 2. Quotations, English. I. Title.
  PN6084.W6A66   1995
  081—dc20

                                                     95-33986
                                                        CIP

ISBN 978-1-250-09631-9 (hardcover)

ISBN 978-1-250-09632-6 (e-book)

Our books may be purchased in bulk for promotional, educational, or business use. Please contact your local bookseller or the Macmillan Corporate and Premium Sales Department at 1-800-221-7945, extension 5442, or by e-mail at MacmillanSpecialMarkets@macmillan.com.

Second Edition: April 2017

10 9 8 7 6 5 4 3 2 1

In loving memory of my mother,

Helen Leona Keyzer Conway,

and for my sweet daughter,

Leah Helen Appel

Introduction

A few weeks after my daughter was born, I was pacing the floors at 2 A.M., trying to bring some comfort to my colicky baby. Walking by our large patio doors, I glanced outside. In the dim light, my reflection in the glass made it appear as if there were three or four of me, receding back into the night. My mother had died the year before, and with her had gone any words of advice about caring for a newborn. Yet in this strange reflection, it seemed as if she were standing there with me, with her mother looking over her shoulder, stretching on into infinity, mom after mom, watching over me. In that moment, I understood that she was there and always would be. Her spirit, her warmth, and her loving ways would guide me as I cared for my child. I was not alone in my motherhood.

Now both my daughter and son are adults, but throughout their lives I have heard my own mother's words of advice and love in the things I have said to them. "Be positive and the world will come to you." "Remember to make your bed before you leave your room in the morning." And, of course, "You are the most wonderful daughter and son in the whole world."

I wish my mother could have lived to see my children. I would have loved to share with her my "mothering" discoveries. Now I understand the reasons behind her anxieties about us, especially one that really drove us crazy. When we were growing up, to our annoyance, she always had to know where we were—which friends, which store, which movie theater. And, later, when we were old enough to travel, we always had to call and let her know we had arrived safely. By the time we were out of college, this behavior seemed ridiculous. But now that I am a mother, I understand completely. It doesn't seem a bit strange. I would like her to know this, and to know that I ask the same of my children, and probably will continue to do so until they have children of their own. They are extensions of me, and just as I have to know where my hands and feet are, I have to know where my children are. They are part of me.

Mothers and daughters have always had interesting relationships. My mother was thirty-nine when she had me, which was unusual in those times. I was her fourth child, and she had run through a lot of childrearing by the time I came along. My brother (who was born three years later) and I provided her with many challenges. But there was one constant that never changed. Through all the admonitions and all the advice, in fact probably *because* of the admonitions and the advice, all of us knew that we were loved, and loved deeply. It was the best lesson she ever taught us.

It should come as no surprise to me that many of the women I know have such strong and resilient mothers. We learned from the best of them—to face life fully, heads held high, savoring the moment at every opportunity. We have forged ahead in life, facing all kinds of obstacles but always moving forward, often with our mother's words ringing in our heads.

One of the best things about editing this book is that I am able to share so many wonderful stories of these remarkable women and the advice they have passed. What a blessing they have been to us!

—*Sherry Appel*

Life

Mother knows best.

When in doubt, ask your momma.

Trust yourself.

*A*lways treat people as if they may someday be on your jury.

Remember that you are known by the company you keep; so always surround yourself with people of good character.

There is absolutely nothing you can't do. (But you may have to give up something else to do it.)

$\mathcal{M}$y mother, Momma J, believes in mercy. Her life has been full of it, giving and receiving. A friend of mine got me a pillow last year that has "Mercy" on it. The word has many meanings but to me, it will always be my mother's greatest gift—her mercy and goodness. Her love of life, her faith, her toughness, and her softness. I'll never be as good as she is, but I aspire to always be better.

—*Terri Johnson*

$\mathcal{O}$ffering kindness and showing gratitude to others can get you through your toughest times.

Let the light inside be light outside.

Don't let the fear of striking out keep you from playing the game.

$\mathcal{G}$rowing up, my mom always told me that "a candle loses no light by lighting another." Through this image and the way she lived her life, she ingrained in me that it is always the right thing to do to help others feel good and do well in life—it does not take away from your own success at all.

—*Tawney Chritton*

$\mathcal{M}$y mother taught me the importance of devotion to family. She taught me to believe that I could do anything I put my mind to. When her friends asked, "Lillian, did you teach Lee to cook?" she would reply, "Hell no, I taught her to read."

She lived her life in such a way that I knew clearly what was valuable and what was not. While bedridden—unable to read or walk—she would say, "Honey, growing old ain't for sissies."

—*Lee Lacy*

Plan ahead.

Try to think of all sides of a question. Intelligence
without understanding is jade without the
carving—just a rock.

If you don't like the results, change the game. If
you can't be Miss Universe, try to be the smartest
nuclear physicist—it's all the category
you choose to compete in.

$\mathcal{F}$ailure is not falling down;
failure is not getting up.

If you tried, you didn't fail.

When you fall, pick up something
while you're down there.

Don't get so big you forget where
you come from.

You pass this way but once.
Any good you can do, do it now.

$\mathcal{N}$o one will believe in you
if you don't believe in yourself first.

My mother was a gem. She always told us not to be quitters. In seventh grade, our school was holding cheerleading tryouts, so a friend and I practiced and practiced. The morning of the tryouts, my friend called to say that she thought we didn't have a chance, so she was not going to try. My mother said, "If you don't try out, you will never know." I did our routine solo and made cheerleader. Her encouragement meant the difference.

—*Susan Conway Himes*

$\mathcal{D}$on't say no very often,
but when you do, mean it.

Be tolerant. Everyone has talent.
Everyone is different.

If you believe something is impossible, it will be.

If something needs to be done,
do it as soon as you notice it.

If you are always getting ready to do something,
it will never get done.

Nothing is taken from you that you cannot learn to live without. (This was Mom's comment when we broke or lost something.)

If you need the rain, you've got to put up with all the thunder and lightning that comes with it.

Don't forget that you're in charge of your life.
If you have a problem, deal with it right away.
Never hide from your problems; they won't
disappear all by themselves.

A smile and a thank-you won't cost you a dime.
But not doing either may cost you later.

My mother, Ho Po-Lan, taught by telling anecdotes and stories that tied us to our Chinese heritage. The message was that to be Chinese, female, and intelligent was often painful. Despite this, all my mother's women friends seemed to have titanium cores. There was always laughter overlaying their sadness.

—*Terry Jones*

Be brave. Timid people never
amount to very much.

It's just as bad to doubt everything
as it is to believe it.

Be careful what you ask for, you may get it.

Be your own woman. Don't waste your time
comparing yourself to others.

Be with, be for—but not against.

Always carry a book.

Don't believe everything you read online or
in the newspaper.

$\mathcal{D}$on't ask other people to do things for you
that you can do for yourself.

If you don't ask questions, you're never
going to learn.

The first hundred years and the first million
dollars are the hardest.

Facebook lasts forever.

If you want people to think you're smart,
learn to listen.

Don't listen to other people's secrets. They always
expect you to tell them yours in return.

Learn to do things for yourself (sew on a button,
change the oil) but always appreciate someone's
offer to do it for you.

$\mathcal{P}$roblems always look smaller after a warm
meal (and a glass of wine) and a
good night's sleep.

Slow down; don't be in such a hurry. It
doesn't do any good to run if you're headed
down the wrong road.

Don't spend time worrying about things
you can do nothing about.

Make up your mind. If you try to sit between two
seats, you're going to end up on the ground.

$\mathcal{O}$ne good way to end up looking foolish is to
pretend you know something you don't.

First impressions go a long way
and last a long time.

If you don't make mistakes,
you don't make anything.

Shoot for the moon.

Never use the truth to hurt someone.

Don't say that something isn't good, say you don't like it or it just doesn't work for you. There's an important difference.

If you're going to have trouble, better to have it
at the beginning than at the end.

Wait until nightfall before saying
it's been a good day.

If you want something more than anything, be
prepared to stake everything.

$\mathcal{I}$f you learn things when you're young, you'll remember them when you're old.

I remember my Aunty Gwen teaching me how to take eggs from under a sitting hen. I used to undertake the task with trepidation since the hens would always peck me to bits. The lesson, basically, consisted of setting your sights on where you thought the eggs would be, taking a deep breath, and shoving your hand quickly and firmly under the hen. Finding that I could do this—after a bit of practice—without any painful retaliation, made me very proud of myself. And even today if I am faced with a prickly problem, I plan my attack, take a deep breath, and plunge forward to reach my goal.

—*Penny Cooper*

Don't think about the cost of doing something;
think about the cost of doing nothing.

If you're lonely or discouraged or unhappy, do
something for someone else.

Always try to be a good sport.

If you're not good at one thing, keep trying.
You're bound to be good at something, even if
you haven't figured it out yet.

Finish what you start.

Keep your eye on the ball.

$\mathcal{M}$y mother taught me that we are not in the world alone, that we are responsible for more than ourselves.

When we plant marigolds in the backyard, we are obliged to care for them, to water them, and to weed them so they have enough space and air and light to grow.

I learned that love entails obligation, that respect must be earned, and that "please" and "thank you" are not simply words to be mumbled at birthday parties.

My mother taught me to be a person.

—*Margot J. Fromer*

$\mathcal{E}$very question doesn't necessarily deserve an answer. And some questions don't have any good answers.

Being a woman should never stop you from anything you want.

Manners

Keep your elbows off the table.

Save room for dinner.

Learn to use a finger bowl, just in case.

Don't have different sets of manners for different people. Treat everyone the same.

Growing up, the advice I *hated* most from my mother was, "See the other person's point of view—try to understand." I got this if someone was mean to me, hit me, or was just nasty in general.

A few days ago, I called my daughter Carrie and asked her what advice of mine she remembers. She said she always hated being told always to try to see the other person's side of things.

I guess that proves what goes around comes around.

—Sunday Wynkoop

"Thank you" and "please" are the
keys to everyone's heart.

Always introduce a young person to an older
one, a man to a woman, and a boy to a girl.

If an older person gets on a crowded bus,
stand up and give her or him your seat.

Always write thank-you notes, but never
send store-bought sympathy cards.

$\mathcal{N}$ever say, "Remember me?" to a person. If you have to ask, they usually don't.

Don't put your glass on a table unless there's a coaster. Or use a napkin.

With dips, remember—only one dip per chip.

Have a firm handshake, look people in
the eye when you speak to them, and
give them your full attention.

Learn to tolerate others' differences: they're not
different from you; you're different from them.

Children and Family

Treat your children like plants—with lots of
sunshine and room to grow.

Read to your children every night
and they'll be readers for life.

Eat with your children. It's the best way
to learn what's going on in their lives.

Always see that your children have
something to look forward to.

Two children is a perfect number, but it would be
terribly hard to stop unless you had a daughter.

Try to make each child feel special. Whenever
a baby is born into a family, be sure to bring a
little gift for the other siblings.

$\mathcal{Y}$ou don't always have to like your siblings,
but you must always love them.

I would always ask my children to call
when they arrived home. Now they insist
I call them on my arrival home.

Don't let your toddlers spend too much
time with digital games; they need
face time and talk time with you.

Hug and kiss your baby every day.

. . . .

$\mathcal{I}$f you don't know right from wrong by the time you're fourteen, then I haven't done my job.

(To my kids when they are skiing): If you don't fall, you're not trying hard enough.

As a teenager, if I ever started to say to my father, "I don't mean to be disrespectful, but . . ." my mother would stop me in my tracks and say, "Then don't be." It's a lesson I used with my own children, and now with my grandchildren.
—*Dawn Ackerman*

. . . .

My mom, Lillian Alexander, taught me the importance of the family meal. Every day, no matter what, there was dinner on the table—the only time of day we would all come together. Simple or elaborate, gourmet or basic, we would sit, eat together, talk together, and bond together. Her mother did this for her, my mother did it for me, and I do it for my family. Food indeed can be love.

When I was four, my mother wrote me a note:

My Dear:

Don't hurry so;
There's ample time.
Why must you rush?
At four, your little legs
can scarcely make the pace
you set for them.
Start now to temper life, while yet a child.
— *Ruth Rice Crone*

Put baby oil on Band-Aids and let them sit for ten minutes. They come off without an "ouch."

Buy children's clothes big.

Be sure you count the Easter eggs before you hide them.

𝖂rite down the funny things your kids say as soon as they say them. Otherwise you'll forget.

Start exposing your kids to culture
(theater, elegant restaurants, New York City)
at a very young age.

Don't name your child something too unusual;
they'll probably get a nickname you'll hate. But
don't pick a name from the top ten either or
there'll be hard times in kindergarten.

"Try a little taste of everything." My mother was a trained dietitian, so our diet was healthy. We had to eat at least one bite of everything. I still enjoy the tasting. . . .

—*Kit Kowalke*

When making peanut butter and jelly sandwiches, always put peanut butter on both sides of the bread and the jelly in the middle. That way the sandwich doesn't get soggy.

If you can't be there when your teenagers come home from school, keep the lights on, and leave a note and an interesting snack.

You're never too old to sit on your mother's lap.

Family comes first.

Never discuss family problems
with the neighbors.

Always stick up for your brothers and sisters.

No matter where you go or what you do, home
is always there for you to come back to.

One of the best Halloween costumes my mother ever made was turning my older brother into a tube of toothpaste. Today this seems almost prophetic since he ultimately chose dentistry as a profession!

—*Beth Della-Bella*

Children want limits: limits make them feel safe.

There is no greater love than that
of a mother for her child.

Having a daughter is a wonderful treasure;
mothers and daughters can be best friends.

Health

*F*or an upset stomach, ginger ale and saltine crackers in small doses are hard to beat.

As a child, my mother instilled in me a love of reading. In the eighth grade, I remember being home sick and reading *Exodus* by Leon Uris. She told me she was going to send a note to school saying I was home "sick in bed with Exodus."

—*Anne F. Ridgely*

Exercise every day. If you don't have time to work out, run the sweeper to the Rolling Stones.

Every once in a while you may need to take a mental health day: call in sick to work, skip class, get a sitter for the kids, and take off—it doesn't matter whether you go to the beach or just drive around listening to your favorite radio station. The important thing is to get time to yourself.

$\mathcal{D}$rink a lot of water, it makes your
skin glow and keeps you healthy.

If your doctor prescribes a medicine and you
take it for two days and don't feel any better,
it's probably the wrong medicine.

Change the batteries in your smoke detectors
every January, whether they need it or not.

A woman can greatly reduce her incidence
of heart attacks and strokes by eating
carrots, spinach, and apricots.

Turning off the cell phone for one hour will actually reduce your stress.

Even if you don't love the taste, eat fruits and vegetables every day. Your body will thank you in twenty years.

Don't forget to put sunscreen on the backs of your hands.

When my mom turned eighty, I presented her with a list of the ten lessons she taught me. When she turned ninety-two, I gave it to her again. She has dementia and is in an assisted-living home. She rarely speaks but can read when prompted, so I asked her to read it to me. She didn't miss a word. When I asked her to skip a few, she asked, "Don't you want me to read all of it?" Her mind and heart and smile are still working, but her brain doesn't connect to her ability to speak on her own. This special moment, however, proved that with the right inspiration and love and stimulation, anything and everything is possible. A moment I will cherish forever. God is good.

—*Debbie Shellenback*

$\mathcal{M}$y mother was more complex than I was. Any woman who would get a divorce during the Depression with two children to raise must have wanted it badly.

She had no hobbies or time for anything but work. She used to insist, "You are not to smoke." And of course I did.

—*Irene T. Appel*

Eat *all* your vegetables.

Always wear a big hat at the beach. It protects your skin and makes you feel very seductive.

Fashion and Clothing

Always shop at the sales rack first.

If you can afford only one good evening dress, get it in black, and buy five pairs of really stunning earrings to change the look.

When you get dressed up, put on everything you want, just the way you want it. Then take off one thing. (Preferably not the dress.)

My mother was one of nine daughters born to Polish immigrants. She married young and lost her husband at a very young age. She raised three daughters on her own. The most descriptive word I can think of to describe her is "generous." Just retired, she recently complained that she was having trouble finding the six-inch red heels for dancing the polka.

—*Patricia Meronoff*

When you get home at night, always change your
shoes. It will give you extra energy
and make the shoes last longer.

Never wear the same pair of shoes
two days in a row.

$\mathcal{A}$ smile is one of the best things
a girl can put on.

Trends come and go, but your style can last
forever if you carry it with confidence.

A black turtleneck, black jeans, and a nice piece
of jewelry can almost take you anywhere—high
heels or boots, your choice.

Just because something is in fashion
does not mean it works for you. Be confident
in your own style.

$\mathcal{I}$f you don't love it in the store,
you'll never wear it.

Mom jeans were never cool and they still aren't.

If you ever find the perfect bra, buy six.

Make sure there's a cotton crotch.

$\mathcal{T}$he power of my mother's words became very obvious to me ten years ago when I was involved in a very serious car crash. As I lay in the car bleeding, with several broken limbs and in severe shock, my first conscious thought was, "My God, what underwear did I wear?"

The first EMS technician ran up, and, to see how badly I was injured, asked me what my name was.

I replied, "Underwear."

The poor man thought I was in a lot worse shape than I really was.

—Pam Beer

Masking tape can work wonders
for an errant hem.

Make sure you know what you
look like from the back.

When you pack a bag for a trip, put in everything that you want. Then take two things out before you close it.

Wearing black always makes you look thinner.

Get the setting of your rings checked every year.

Cooking and Entertaining

$\mathcal{I}$f you can read, you can cook.

All good cooks burn (or cut) themselves
every once in a while.

Clean up as you cook.

No soda or other bottles of any kind at the table.

Pass the salt and pepper at the same time.

Cold food always needs more
salt than warm food.

When using a microwave, add salt
and pepper after cooking.

Don't have a children's table; you can
have two tables but mix up the ages.
You'll all learn something.

You may not like to cook, but learn to make three great dishes, one fabulous dessert, and how to scramble an egg. The Internet will show you how.

Don't make things too complicated; prep ahead of time so you can be with your guests.

Relax. There is nothing more uncomfortable than a nervous host.

For the last few years of her life, my mother was in poor health. At one point, she was unable to eat. In despair, her doctors sent her home, thinking perhaps my cooking might appeal to her. My husband and I made our very best meals, but a few bites were all she could manage. Then one day, my mother got out of bed and prepared an enormous and delicious meal and ate quite a bit of it, too. We didn't do any more cooking for her.

—*Susan Darter Hunt*

*N*ever slam a door when you have a cake or
a soufflé in the oven, as it may fall.

Knead your biscuit with a light hand or
you'll have stones for dinner.

Never roll out a piecrust more than once.
If you do, it will be as tough as nails.

Don't wash mushrooms before you put them in the refrigerator. And store them in paper bags.

Always start bacon in a cold pan.

When making applesauce, use as many different types of apples as possible.

When cooking with tomatoes, always add a pinch of sugar.

$\mathcal{I}$f you want to have a successful party, plan the food and decorations around a theme and play great music—loud.

At parties, shake hands and mingle. Remember, guests have a responsibility to make a party work.

Choose between having two drinks before dinner or wine with the meal. If you have both you probably will regret it the next day.

If your house looks reasonably neat, it doesn't have to be spotless. If company comes, turn off as many lights as possible and use a lot of candles.

Food should look as beautiful as possible when you serve it. Every day.

Home

$\mathcal{P}$lants die—buy new ones.

Big plants are easier to care for than small ones.

Water your overhead hanging plants by
putting a few ice cubes in the pot.

Always set a time for dinner.
Breakfast and lunch can be at any time at all.

It is not a sign of weakness to use paper plates.

When arranging flowers, add in stems from
any herb growing in the garden—flowering
oregano, chive blossoms, purple basil, or mint
work well and add to the overall scent.

My mom loves creating inviting "moments." Whenever she was having people over, welcoming me home from college, or just needed a little pick-me-up, she would arrange a charming scene on the kitchen counter with a whimsical tea towel, a vase of fresh flowers, and a white candle in an amber glass holder. She would put a few stems in a small vase by my bed as well, and spray fresh lavender mist on my pillows and sheets.

—*Tawney Chritton*

My mom always admonished me for worrying about cleaning my house and running the vacuum so much. Her final word on the subject was usually, "No one ever wanted to have 'She kept a clean house' on her tombstone."

—*Anne F. Ridgely*

Separate the lights from the darks.

Don't put your bras in the dryer.

Put a load of laundry in the washer when you
leave for work, move it to the dryer
when you come home.

Buy dark towels.

$\mathcal{M}$y mother bought an artificial Christmas tree and after a number of tears setting the tree up and taking it down, she simply decided to put a large green plastic bag over it, and leave it in a corner of the family room. Then presto, the next Christmas (or any time, for that matter), she took the green plastic bag off and we were ready for our celebration! She said that this made Christmas easier, and that allowed more time for other things.

—*Patty Craley*

Always put the tinsel on the Christmas
tree one piece at a time.

$\mathcal{C}$lean up spilt milk very carefully
or it will smell.

Always make your bed before
leaving the house.

What makes a room beautiful is not the
furniture or the flowers or paintings
but light, and you can do a lot of
that yourself by painting the whole
place white. Off-white. A very
slightly warm white is best.

Put everything in its own place and
you'll always know where everything is.

Put fabric softener sheets in your teenage son's
sneakers to keep them from getting too ripe.

In sewing, it's the finishing that counts.
Always make a nice hem.

Keep a magnet in your sewing box
to help pick up dropped needles.

Cut your thread on an angle and
it will be easier to thread onto a needle.

It's no use saying, "Don't get a dog." But don't get a dog until your children are old enough to walk him.

Three or four months is a good age to get a puppy. But you don't need to get him from a kennel.

Money

Always take out a line of credit
before you need it.

Do with what you have;
don't borrow from anyone.

Never buy anything at full price.

Even putting aside $25 every other week into
your 401(k) is important. Compound interest can
work small miracles given enough time.

$\mathcal{M}$om took care of the little things, like shopping, cooking, cleaning, laundry, and making sure my brother, father, and I had everything we needed. Before my father passed away, Mom had never written a check. Now she balances her checkbooks, takes care of all the bills, runs the house, and takes the car for oil changes and maintenance. I admire her grit, her ability to pick up the pieces of her life, and her independence.

—*Beverly R. Silverberg*

Husbands and wives should pool their material belongings into "ours," rather than separating them into "mine." It makes for an easier and healthier relationship.

Never go grocery shopping when you're hungry.

Plain old petroleum jelly is just as
good as the expensive stuff.

Turn out the light when you leave a room.
It sounds silly to a child, but added up over
a year it can save you money.

$\mathcal{B}$uying cheap is always a waste of money.

Never skimp when you're buying leather goods; you'll never have to replace a good quality handbag and you'll end up saving in the long run.

Pay the balance on your credit card every month.

Always keep your receipts.

Keeping Up Appearances

You don't have to be beautiful;
you just have to walk as if you were.

Always stand up straight; you'll feel more
powerful and your clothes will fit better.

Remember that presentation counts—in food,
in your work, and in yourself.

$\mathcal{I}$f your hair looks nice and your shoes look nice, whatever you're wearing will look nice, too.

Always check your makeup in a light different from where you applied it.

Put your feet together when you're having your picture taken.

Too many cocktails can dry out the skin.

Smoking gives you age lines.

$\mathcal{A}$lways carry a handkerchief or
a pack of tissues.

Learn to dance.

My grandmother was a constant source of spunk and wit. Even after suffering a major heart attack, she maintained her sense of humor. While I was visiting her in the hospital, her cardiologist commented on our resemblance. Grandma pointed out (much to this fourteen-year-old's embarrassment) I even had bowlegs. "However," Grandma continued, "we'd rather call them 'Pleasure Bent.' "

—*Nancy Fissel Hauser*

Comb your eyebrows.

Brush your tongue.

When you really feel down, buy the reddest lip-stick you can find.

Beauty takes pains.

Keep current on your pedicures.

My mother had more than her share of hardships in her life, but she always believed in showing her best face to the world. In mother-daughter code that translated in her admonishment to me, "Honey, you need a little lipstick." Whatever disappointment, worry, or annoyance I might have been experiencing, she expected me to put on a happy face, and get on with life.

—*Sunny Mays Schust*

$\mathcal{T}$aking care of your skin is not a luxury;
it's an investment that will keep increasing in
value the older you get.

When I would go out in my early twenties, my
mother used to always say to me, "A wasted mind
and body has no owner." Mind you, this was in
Spanish, so I'm roughly translating. It was her way
to warn me that if you drink too much, you lose
control of your mind and body and anyone can do
anything to you.

—*Natalia Martinez*

Friendship

Ain't nobody your best friend
like your momma.

"Remember well and bear in mind, a trusty friend
is hard to find." Inscription in a charm bracelet, a
gift to my mother from her sister.
—*Peggy A. Cavender*

If you play music, you will never be alone.

$\mathcal{R}$emember to have fun, just not
at someone else's expense.

Make friends with people who
encourage and inspire you.

Don't do things for people just because
you feel sorry for them.

My mother was wise in many ways. When I was very little, she heard me playing "church" in my room. Apparently, God was in the class and misbehaving, whereupon I told God to "sit down and shut up." Her first thought was to tell me not to talk to God in that way, and then she thought it was better that I had such a close and friendly relationship with the deity.

—*Pam Beer*

When you go to the hospital to have your baby, don't have your best friend take care of your husband while you're gone.

When a friend breaks up with her boyfriend, never say anything bad about him. She may fall in love with him again.

Never be the one to give a friend bad news about a husband or boyfriend. Someone else, usually an enemy, will always do that job.

$\mathcal{N}$ever room with a close friend. It's the best way to destroy a friendship.

A sure way to lose a friend is to loan her money or clothing you really care about.

When my roommate had worn me out with her romantic woes, I finally bet her that she wouldn't think about *him* if she starved herself. I was amazed. She lasted twenty-four hours before deciding that her only thought was for a grilled cheese.

— *Terry Jones*

Love, Men, Relationships

Don't do anything at night that you'll
feel bad about in the morning.

Don't marry a man you think
you're going to change.

$\mathcal{B}$efore marriage, keep your eyes wide open.
After marriage, keep them half shut.

Relationships aren't 50-50. If you expect
100 percent of someone's love, you
must give 100 percent of yourself.

Take half the credit and half the blame
for any misunderstanding.

You can marry more money in a minute
than you can make in a lifetime.

It doesn't matter whether you marry a rich man
or a poor man: money comes and goes. It's
intelligence and ambition that stick around.

$\mathcal{D}$on't go fishing in a man's belongings, especially his cell phone, because you just might find what you were looking for.

If you can take a beau away from another woman, then someone else will be able to take him away from you.

Don't blame the ocean because you haven't caught any fish.

If you're always depending on men, you're always going to be disappointed.

$\mathcal{F}$ind a man who is crazy about you and make him your best friend. I did! I consider myself the luckiest woman alive to be married to my husband.

—*Mary Hendley*

Always look good for your husband.

Love is very important, but your husband also likes you because you make him laugh.

How a man treats his mother is a clear
indication of how he treats his wife.

Never marry a man who is
still living with his mother.

You don't have to get married.

Remember who you are.

Going through difficult times with your partner is not a bad thing. It is a true test of character.

Regarding a broken heart, my aunt, Loly Henriquez, used to tell me that no matter how intense the love you shared, when you break up, the sting lasts three months. After that, your heart will become stronger and the healing speeds up.

—*Natalia Martinez*

$\mathcal{A}$ll through high school and college my mom told me, "Don't worry about dating—figure out what you like to do and find a way to make that your career path." Here I am all these years later doing what I love and married to my best friend—not having suffered through a bunch of relationships that didn't serve me or my career. On my wedding day, I told her she was right and thanked her for that advice.

—*Ashley Kerns*

In an older era, a young woman would be advised to "take a long hat pin and mad money" on a date, just in case. These days, it may be wise to keep your Uber account up-to-date if a fast getaway is needed.

Don't think that your love will change a man. Most people can't change and don't want to anyway.

After you get married, don't iron the first shirt. Let him do it himself.

Do you want me to punch the other arm
so that one doesn't hurt so much?

The best men walk on their toes.

Never go out with a guy whose belt
buckle is bigger than his head.

Weddings

Never get a wedding present monogrammed until after the wedding.

Ask someone to keep track of all the wedding presents, cards, etc. Otherwise writing thank-you notes will be a nightmare.

Don't have a friend take the wedding pictures. Hire a professional.

$\mathcal{B}$lankets are good wedding presents. It may not seem very exciting to the bride and groom, but they'll remember you in the years to come every time they get the blanket out to make up a guest bed.

When you're in the middle of planning a wedding and everything seems impossible, just keep in mind that all you really need is the guy you're going to marry and a minister/rabbi/judge. The essentials are easy and the details are ultimately unimportant.

Remember: most weddings only take twenty minutes.

The morning of my wedding, Mother rather hesitantly shared with me a family tradition. She gave me fifty dollars in cash, which I was to keep on hand so that "I could always come home." The airline fare from Washington, D.C., to Springfield, Illinois, was fifty dollars at the time. She explained that all the women in our family (presumably she herself and my sister) always relied on this insurance.

—*Ellen M. Bozman*

Work and Education

All my life, I remember my mother and aunts telling me about being awakened on Monday morning by their mother with, "Wake up, it's Monday. Tomorrow is Tuesday, then Wednesday, and the week is half gone already and we've got nothing done!"

—*Kathryn Herrod Letson*

Make decisions in the morning; that's when your brain is at its sharpest.

Bessie Bowling Morse was born on February 2, 1903, and was raised in Nelson County, Virginia. She was the youngest of eight children. She worked as a maid and then as a companion for two of the richest white families in Nelson County most of her life. She was the first black woman to drive a Model T Ford.

—*Shirley Clark*

If you can read, you can do anything.

$\mathcal{U}$se your imagination.

Be flexible.

Take notes.

You always get your best ideas in the shower,
in the middle of the night, or driving to work.
Keep pen and paper handy to write them down
immediately! (You will *not* remember them later.)

If you're not the lead dog,
the scenery never changes.

If you're supposed to be the leader, make sure
what direction you're heading in before you start.

The advice that rings through my memory is, "Be a
leader, not a follower." Sometimes that was difficult to
follow through on, but in the end it always paid off. The
highest tribute I could pay my mother is that I am trying
to be a woman I believe she is.

—*Gail Pennybacker Rose*

Act as if you will always succeed.

If you ask people for the impossible,
you'll get the best possible.

Always act like the winner when you lose.

Just because the surface of the pond is
calm doesn't mean there aren't
crocodiles waiting underneath.

My mom often told me to "rise above it" when I was growing up. Little did my mother know that this simple saying would act as a seed in my life, sowing confidence, humility, and strength. Even today, I am often in situations in which I need to displace myself for a moment, reflect on "rising above it," and choose to act on this wisdom.

—*Amy O. Ryan*

If you're going to complain, always complain to
the person who can help you.

Divide any big job into a succession of small jobs.

Never start the next thing before finishing
the first thing.

Find a job or profession that brings you joy.

Sometimes one phone call is worth
a hundred text messages.

Never write and send an e-mail when you're
angry. Write, wait overnight, and then
delete it in the morning.

Read over your e-mails twice
before sending them.

Widowed at thirty-four with two small children, my mother was faced with the inevitable question of how could she possibly go on. She set out with blinders of steel and her journey was one of formidable strength and determination. The two traits I inherited from her: laughter and silent thought. The first: being able to laugh, even when it hurts, is one of the greatest therapies of life. The second: thinking through a problem, taking the pieces apart, laying them all out, and then gradually fitting them together to create an answer.

—P. Diane Ferring

$\mathcal{I}$f you can't be good at something,
at least be enthusiastic.

When you deal with the public,
treat everyone equally, rich or poor.

Never make important decisions when
you're angry. Whatever you do will almost
always be wrong. Calm down, then act.

If you have a number of jobs you don't
want to do, do the one you don't want
to do the most first.

If you want to get a job done, ask a busy person.

A thing is only worth so much time.

$\mathcal{N}$ever quit a job before you have another job.

Be careful when making a change. You might be trading one set of problems for another, so be sure that you'll like the new problems better than the old ones.

Don't be afraid of your boss. Better to
ask twice than be wrong once.

If you're the boss, give people the bad news
on Monday, and they'll be too busy during
the week to brood on it. Give them the
good news on Friday, so they can have
the weekend to celebrate.

Don't be afraid to ask for a raise, but
be prepared with a list of your accomplishments
and contributions when you do it.

Never sign anything that you
haven't already read.

Be careful not to promise
anything that you can't deliver.

Decide what you want to be,
then do what you have to do to be it.

With regard to career and motherhood—you
can have it all, just maybe not at the same time.

$\mathcal{D}$on't split infinitives.

Any job, big or small, is worth
doing well or not at all.

Don't try to find opportunity—make it.

Girls can mow lawns, too!

Your mind can concentrate fully on only one thing at a time. Organize your desk to implement that one task. Remove all other distractions.

Pay attention to yourself for a week and see where and how you waste time. Then do something about it.

*D*on't tell people what you're not going
to do or what you would have done.

Education is paramount. Marriage will
always be there if you want it.

Luck is always nice, but it's hard work that
usually gets you what you want, and you
need to want it more than anything.

Be productive, but live life and
have a good time.

Do it now.

My mother is my best friend. Words could never even scratch the surface of my admiration for and devotion to her. She is courageous, adventurous, warm, loving, and beautiful. I know how much I have been blessed, and never let a day go by without thanking God for her.

—*Irene Calabrese*

Special Thanks

We would like to thank the following mothers, daughters, aunts, and grandmothers for their generous contributions to this book. Reading their stories of joy, pain, love, humor, and patience brought us a sincere appreciation for the job of mothering. Many said they enjoyed the opportunity to sit down and write about their moms, or simply spend time thinking about their past relationships. One woman added, "Thanks for this. It felt good." If readers would like to contribute to future books on mothers and advice, you can write to us in care of our terrific editor, BJ Berti, at St. Martin's Press, 175 Fifth Avenue, New York, N.Y. 10010.

Barbara Conway Abbruzzese, Helen Leona Keyzer Conway; Irene Trippett Appel, Emma Busch Mason;

Deirdre Ruckman Appel, Anna Rae Ruckman; Mary Ann Barrows, Daisy L. Meyer; Bonnie Beck; Pam Beer, June F. Beer; Donna Greenfield Belser; Barbara Bode; Ellen M. Bozman; Kellis E. Bunner, Dorothy L . Legg, Dorothy E. Armer; Irene Calabrese, Grazia Calabrese; Elizabeth Force Carson, Patricia L. Force; Linda S. Wernick Cassell, Jeanne Ann Wernick; Peggy A. Cavender, Effie Violet Jordan Cavender; Hilary L. Chiz; Shirley Clark, Bessie Bowling Morse; Penny Cooper, Aunty Gwen Cooper; Caryn Coyle, Claire Norma Stacey Coyle; Patty Craley; Ruth Rice Crone, Thelma Ryle Rice; Ann Davidson, Violet Olson Gunderson; Carol Deal; Mary DelPopolo, Florence Marie Pesanti DelPopolo; Beth Della-Bella, Mary Lou Della-Bella, Phyllis J. Norton; Kathleen Dragan, Helen Toohey; Nancy Duggan; Linda Eads, Eloise Eads, Beaulah W. DeJarnette; Kathleen Ewing, JoAnne Ewing; Yvonne Synder Farley, Malwina Synder; Elizabeth Farrell; Jamie Fear; Jocelyn C. Ferguson, Madeline J. Clark, Nora Clark Davis; Sandy Appel Fisher; Darlene Foster; Barbara Frank, Esther Mindel Frank; Amanda Fisher Fredrickson; Margot J. Fromer; Lisa Garrison; Julie Himes Gerig, Susan Conway Himes; Linda Gray; Karen Elliott Greisdorf, Mary White Elliott; Lynn Gumbowski; Tara Hamilton, Esther Ennis, Patricia King; Geraldine Vickers Harrison, Linnie Faber Vickers; Nancy Fissel Hauser, Mary Fissel, Louise Bensel; Carla Haner; Joy E. Held, Joy Opal Gunnoe Dick; Mary Hendley, Frances Rose Wilson; Charlotte Henline; Debbie Herr; Estelle Forshaw Himes; Susan Darter Hunt, Blanche Boykin Beauregard; Ellen Jaffe, Molly C. Jaffe; Martha Siegfried Johnson, Mary Myrtle Power Siegfried; Patricia A. Jones, Maureen Rose McCormick Jones; Terry Jones, Ho Po-Lan; Karen Kalish, Berta S. Kalish, Estelle W. Kalish; Jodi Jett Karr; Allison E. Kofoet, Judith M. Kofoet; Kit Kowalke; Lee Lacy, Lillian Lam Hitchcock; Robin Latham; Kathryn Herrod Letson, Arrie Etta Herrod; Penny Lewandowski; Denise Lloyd; Karyn T. Lynch; Grace Madole; Allison McCall, Ruth Berke, Lizzie Kobre;

Eugenia (Jean) Kelly McCall, Bridget Gormley Kelly; Susan Clem McKenna, Jane Clem; Bonni McKeown, Virginia-Lou Austin McKeown; Patricia Meronoff, Eleanor Meronoff; Wendy Miller; Jan Mitchell, Mary Ellen Phillips; Evelyn Schietinger Morris, Ruth Evelyn Brock Schietinger; Barbara Moum, Pat Moum; Gladys Peterson Nemecek; Suzanne Ruckman Nowell; Margaret Oppenheimer; Bobbie Seifer Paul, Anne Satterthwaite Seifer, Freda Schultz Seifer, Edith Margerum Satterthwaite; Gail Pennybacker Rose, Dee Pennybacker; Dorothy Conway Pinegar, Sarah Sevier Conway; Margie Polk; Rachel Power, Virgina Power; Carolyn Psai, Dorothy Keswick; Cina Radler, Harriet Radler; Emily Isberg Reardon, Sylvia Waldman Isberg (stage name Sue Bailey); Abigail R. Reynolds, Rachel Ann Reynolds, Talma P. Robertson; Anne F. Ridgely, Helen Marie Rinehart; Jill Ellen Rosenthal, Joyce Karp Lindmark; Stella Katchan Wheeler; Amy O. Ryan, Connie Ryan; Judi Scioli, Rhoda Nisenholtz; Rebecca L. Sheppard, Margaret G. Sheppard; Trudy

Shultz; Beverly R. Silverberg, Anne Gubenko Rabner, Nina Silverberg; Jane Elizabeth Slagter, Edith Elinore McMahan; Elisabeth M. Smeda, Ione M. Hoekenga; Lucye J. Synder, Lillie Ann Rider; Jean Steele; Ruthann R. Stone; Susan Alfandre Swain, Rose Glasser Alfandre; Patricia (Patsy) Ticer, Margaret (Peggy) Keyser Smith; Eileen Toumanoff, Louise Thoron MacVeagh; Alexandra Truitt, Anne Dean Truitt; Patricia Warren, Ida Warren; Alissa Watkins, Maxine Roberts, Margie Bray; Ann Williams White, Sarah Elizabeth Stinnie Williams; Judy Conway Wilgus, Anna Sevier Facey, Nora Brown, Tracy Wilgus Weins; Betty Wilson; Page Winstead, Helen T. Vietor, Marion L. Winstead; Lisa Woo, Rosalie Yee Quil Woo; Sunday Wynkoop, Susan Hammett, Viola Roberts, Carrie Evans Wynkoop

Additional thanks to Dawn Ackerman; Leah Appel; Hannah Baker, Sara Thompson Baker; Tawney Chritton, Kay-Lynn Czarnecki; Deborah Doehr Kim, Barbara Doehr; Barb Eljenholm, Taylor Eljenholm;

· ·

P. Diane Ferring, Clydie Ferring; Terri Johnson, Jeanette Williams Johnson; Ashley Kerns, Linda Kerns; Natalia Martinez, Ana Comayagua, Loly Henriquez; Ann MacFarlane, Aileen MacFarlane; Dana Alexander Nolfe, Lillian Alexander; Frances Penney, Kathleen Linehan Penney; Marion Rozich Pionke; Sunny Mays Schust, Ruthanna Mays; Debbie Shellenback, Evelyn Trent Walker Shaffron; Regina Fraind Smith, Stefany Fraind; Christina Martin Tolley, Lia Martina Tolley, Gail Martin; Sharon Lloyd Young, and Irene Zimmer Young for their contributions to the 2017 edition of this book.